Mozart

Alla Turca
from Sonata K. 331

Cover photography: Copyright © 1999 Randall Wallace
All Rights Reserved.

Project editor: Peter Pickow

Copyright © 1999 by Amsco Publications,
A Division of Music Sales Corporation, New York

Order No. AM 949828
International Standard Book Number: 0.8256.1749.9

Exclusive Distributors:
Music Sales Corporation
257 Park Avenue South, New York, NY 10010 USA
Music Sales Limited
8/9 Frith Street, London W1V 5TZ England
Music Sales Pty. Limited
120 Rothschild Street, Rosebery, Sydney, NSW 2018, Australia

Printed in the United States of America by
Vicks Lithograph and Printing Corporation

Amsco Publications
New York/London/Paris/Sydney/Copenhagen/Madrid

Alla Turca

from Sonata K. 331

Wolfgang Amadeus Mozart